"Our film, I hope, will be a micro-
cosm of New York. It's the glamour of the
Great White Way of Broadway and the
squalor of 42nd Street; the dream of in-
stant success and the constant reminder
of failure; the fine line between a Juilliard
Scholarship and dancing topless at the
Metropole... It's George M. Cohan and
the City Ballet. Rock and Roll and Vivaldi.
It is New York... vulgar and beautiful. A
dozen races pitching in and having their
own crack at the American Dream."

Alan Parker
In his pre-production letter
to the Crew, July 9th, 1979

CONTENTS

FAME   6

DOGS IN THE YARD   20

HOT LUNCH JAM   16

I SING THE BODY ELECTRIC   46

IS IT OKAY IF I CALL YOU MINE?   30

NEVER ALONE   37

OUT HERE ON MY OWN   12

RALPH AND MONTY (DRESSING ROOM PIANO)   44

RED LIGHT   25

Editor: David C. Olsen

FAME

Lyrics by
DEAN PITCHFORD

Music by
MICHAEL GORE

Moderate dance beat ♩ = 132

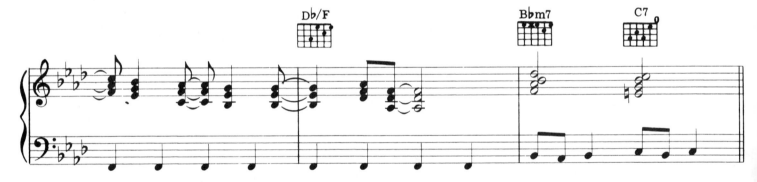

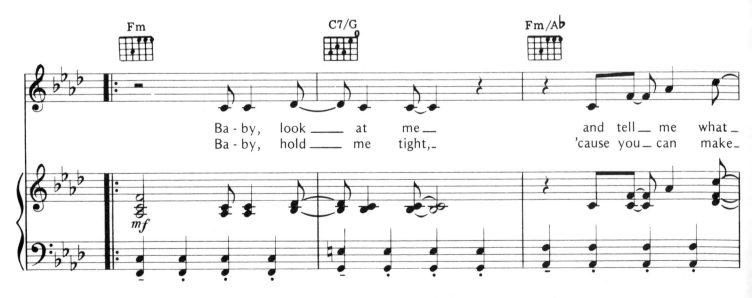

Ba - by, look ___ at me ___ and tell ___ me what ___
Ba - by, hold ___ me tight, ___ 'cause you ___ can make ___

re - mem - ber,　　re - mem - ber.

loco

Db　　Bbm7　　C7

Fm　　Db

Bbm7　　C7　　2. Fm

D.S. ad lib. and fade 𝄋

name,　　fame!

decresc.

OUT HERE ON MY OWN

Lyrics by
LESLEY GORE

Music by
MICHAEL GORE

14

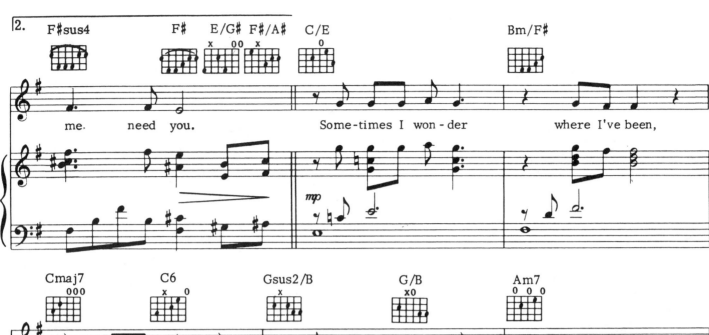

me. need you. Some-times I won-der where I've been,

who I am, do I fit in. I may not win,

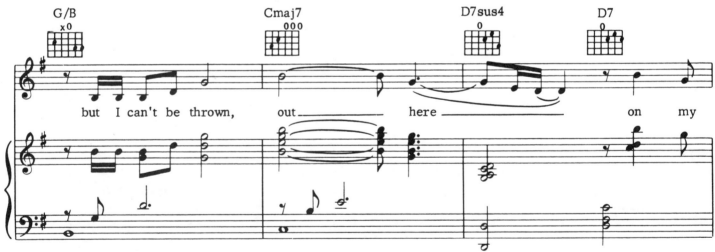

but I can't be thrown, out____ here ____ on my

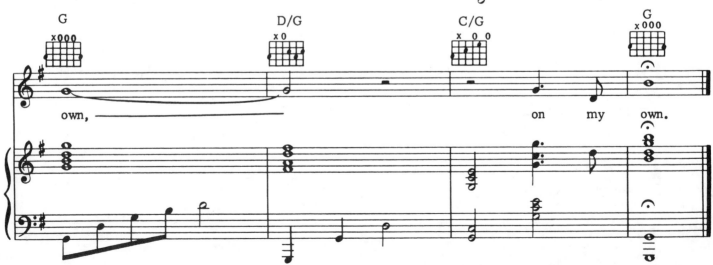

own, ____ on my own.

HOT LUNCH JAM

Lyrics by
LESLEY GORE and ROBERT COLESBERRY

Music by
MICHAEL GORE

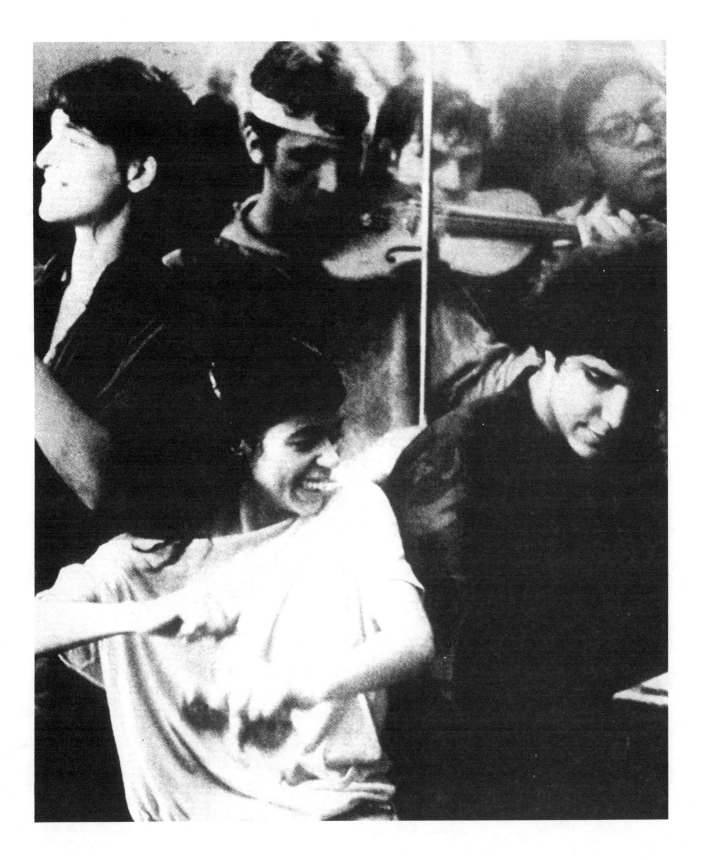

DOGS IN THE YARD

Words and Music by
DOMINIC BUGATTI and FRANK MUSKER

RED LIGHT

Lyrics by
DEAN PITCHFORD

Music by
MICHAEL GORE

I worked so hard to get___ me a man.___ Don't
I don't want you hang - in' a - round.___ My

try   to take him a - way.___   I
man   is too hard to hold.___   But

Cb Db Eb Gb

bad e-nough it could burn ____ you. ____ Red is all I can see. ____

Ab Cb

____ Hot is how it will be; ____ bad for you if you mess ____

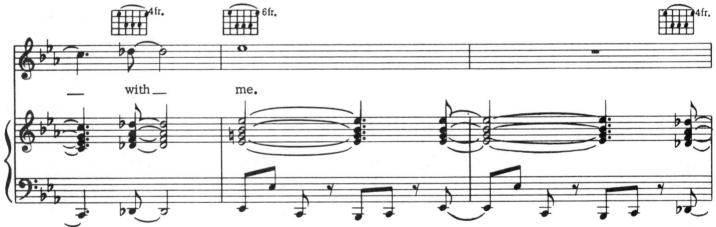

Db Eb Db

____ with ____ me.

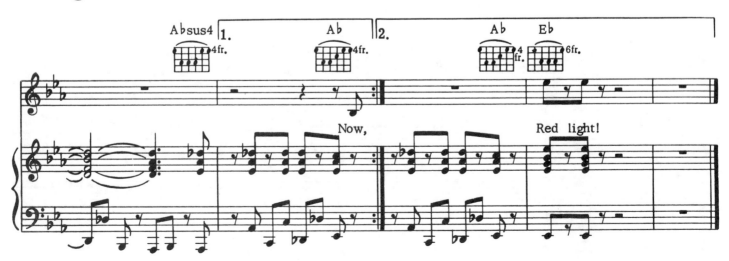

Absus4 1. Ab 2. Ab Eb

Now, Red light!

IS IT OKAY IF I CALL YOU MINE?

Lyrics and Music by
PAUL McCRANE

if I know that you know __ that I'm ____ want-ing,

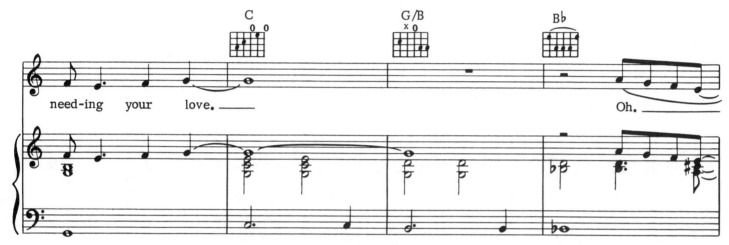

need-ing your love. ____

Oh. ____

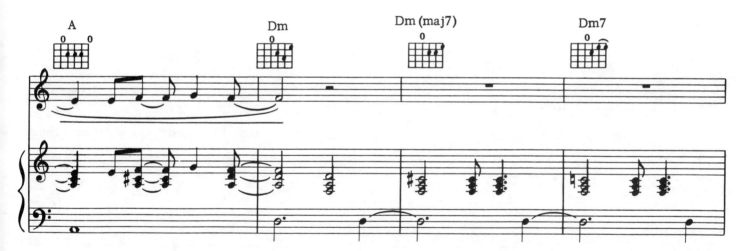

If I ask of you ___ is it all __ right, _

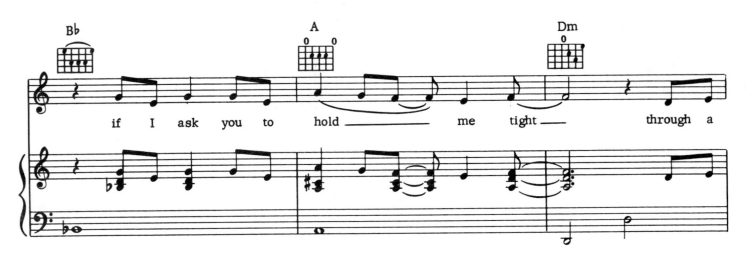

if I ask you to hold _____ me tight ____ through a

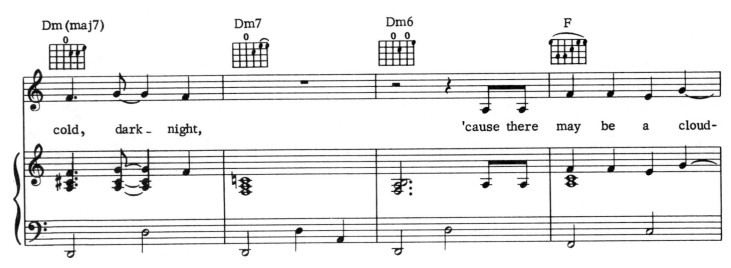

cold, dark_ night, 'cause there may be a cloud-

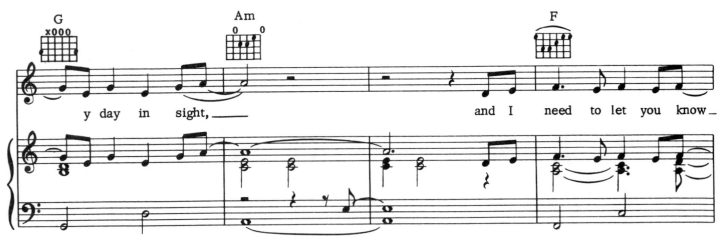

y day in sight, _____ and I need to let you know _

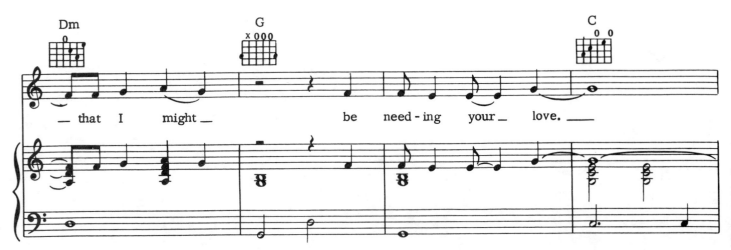

_ that I might _ be need-ing your _ love. ___

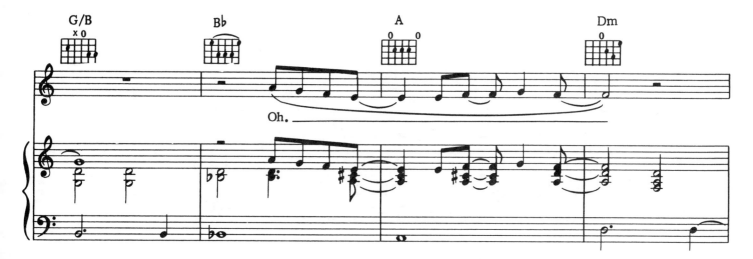

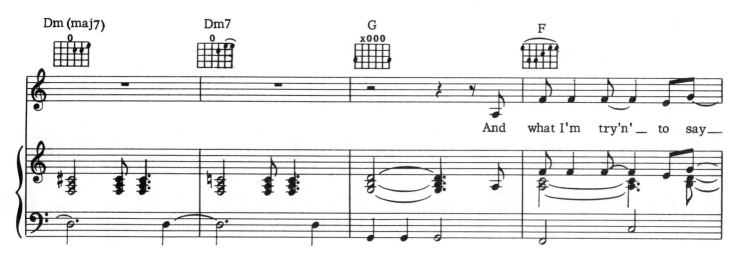

Oh.

And what I'm try'n'_ to say_

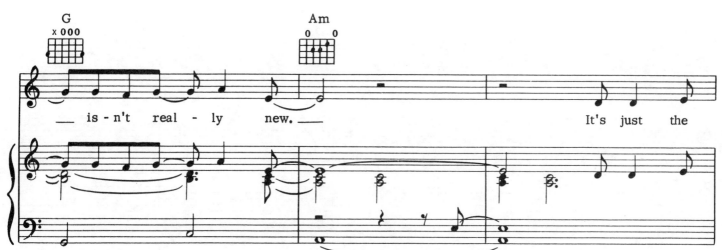

_ is-n't real-ly new. _ It's just the

things that hap-pen to me_ when I'm re-mind-ed of you, like when I

hear your name or see a place that you've been, — or see a pic - ture of — your grin, —

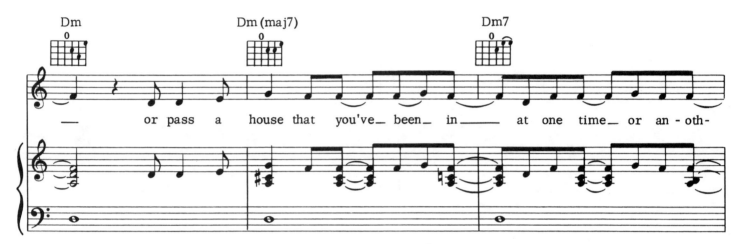

— or pass a house that you've — been — in — at one time — or an - oth-

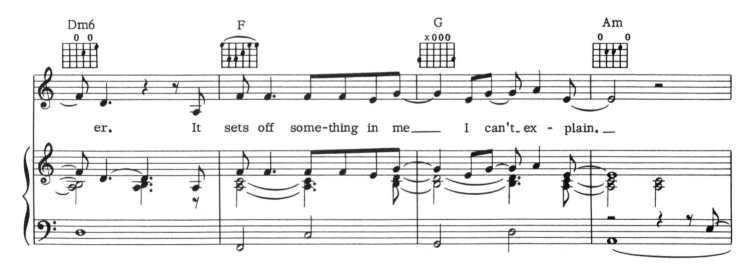

er. It sets off some-thing in me — I can't — ex - plain. —

And I can't wait to see — you — a-gain. Oh, babe, —

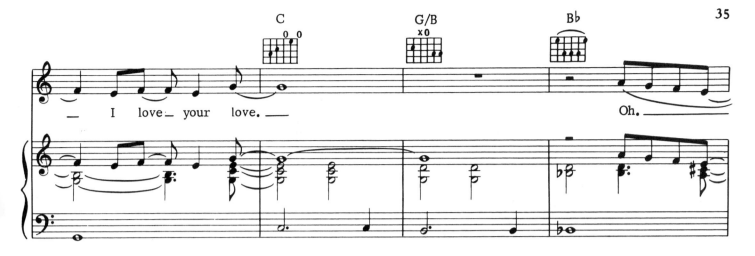

I love your love. Oh. _____

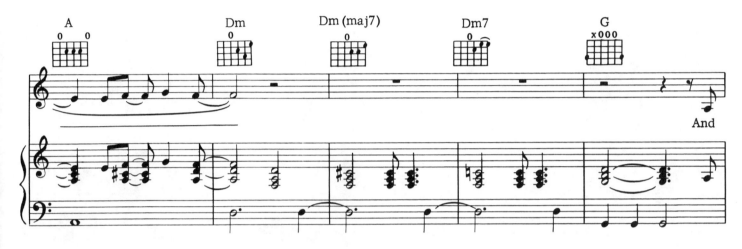

And

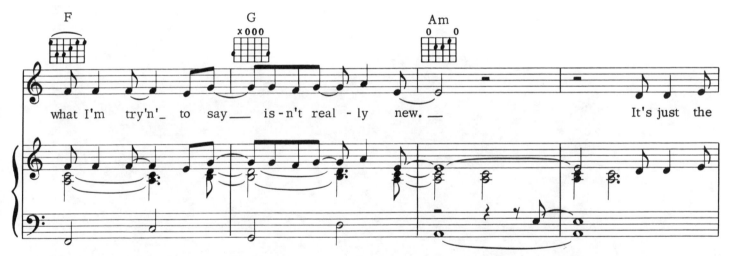

what I'm try'n' to say___ is-n't real-ly new. ___ It's just the

things that hap-pen to me ___ when I'm re-mind-ed of you.

rit.

NEVER ALONE

By
ANTHONY EVANS

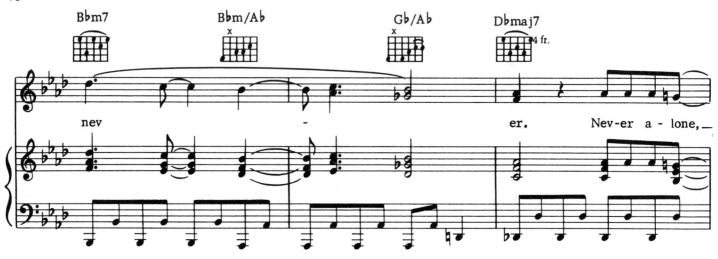

nev - er. Nev-er a - lone,__

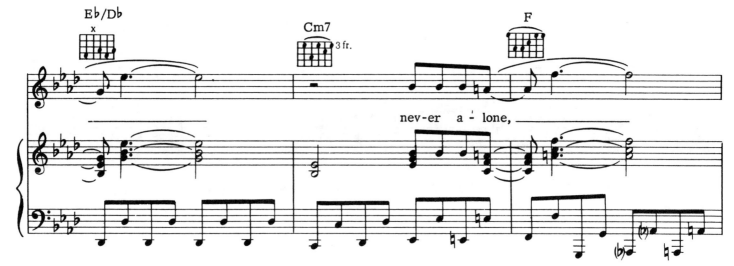

nev-er a - lone,_____

He'll nev - er leave__ you a-

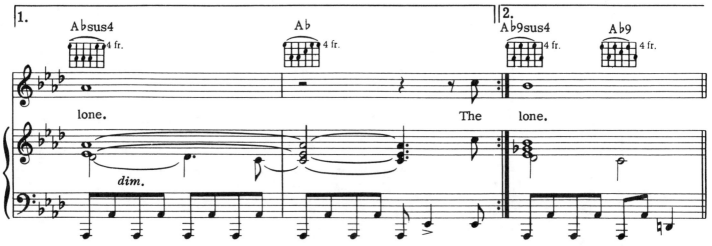

lone.   The lone.

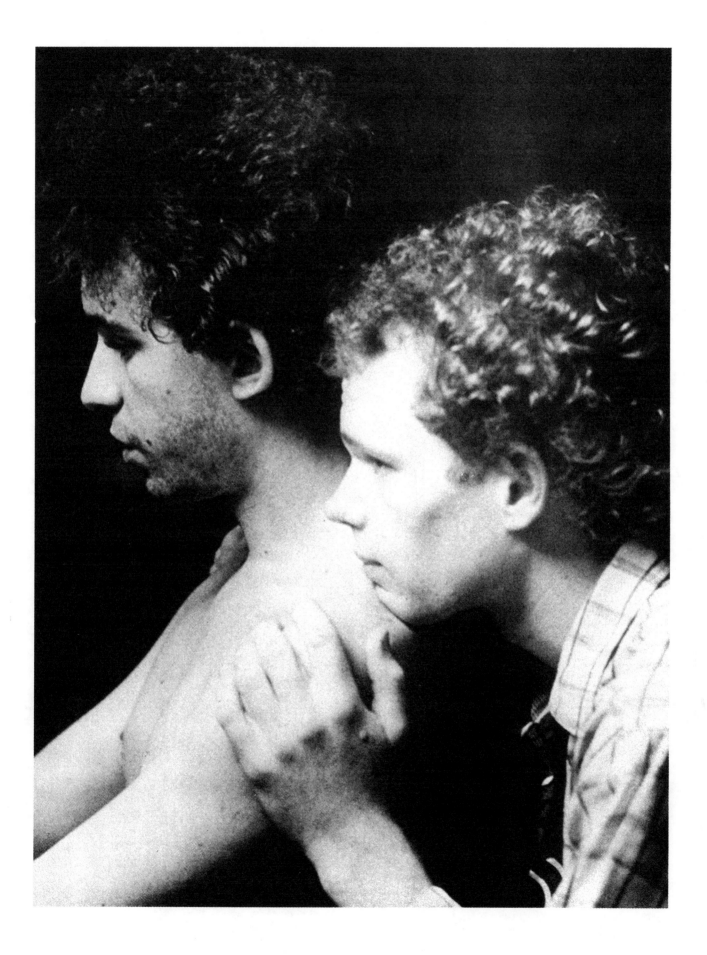

RALPH AND MONTY
(Dressing Room Piano)

By
MICHAEL GORE

Moderately, lyrically

mf espressivo

I SING THE BODY ELECTRIC

Lyrics by
DEAN PITCHFORD

Music by
MICHAEL GORE